FOREST
and its
Wildlife

Also by Geoff Moon:

Auckland Birds and Wildlife
New Zealand High Country and its Wildlife
New Zealand Coast and its Wildlife
New Zealand Offshore Islands and their Wildlife
The Reed Field Guide to New Zealand Birds
The Reed Field Guide to New Zealand Wildlife

REED HABITAT GUIDES 1

New Zealand FOREST *and its* Wildlife

Geoff Moon

Front cover: Kauri forest; morepork (ruru) carrying a weta to its nest hole (inset).

Back cover: Green gecko (top); kauri snail shells (bottom).

Title page: Orbweb spider.

Published by Reed Books, a division of Reed Publishing (NZ) Ltd, 39 Rawene Road, Birkenhead, Auckland 10. Associated companies, branches and representatives throughout the world.

This book is copyright. Except for the purpose of fair reviewing, no part of this publication may be reproduced or transmitted in any form or by any means, electronic or mechanical, including photocopying, recording, or any information storage and retrieval system, without permission in writing from the publisher. Infringers of copyright render themselves liable to prosecution.

Text and photographs © Geoff Moon 1995.

ISBN 0 7900 0426 7

First published 1995

Adapted from *The Reed Field Guide to New Zealand Wildlife* (1995)

Printed in Singapore

CONTENTS

AUTHOR'S NOTE 7

INTRODUCTION 8

NEW ZEALAND FOREST 20
AND ITS WILDLIFE

INDEX 62

Morepork feeding chick.

AUTHOR'S NOTE

In its comparatively small landmass, New Zealand has a wide variety of habitats, providing homes for many interesting creatures, both native and introduced. The most conspicuous forms of wildlife are the birds and insects. Apart from seals, there are no large native wild mammals, and with the exception of the long-tailed bat and the endemic short-tailed bat, all other mammals have been introduced.

This book illustrates the wildlife to be found in the various forest habitats. For more detailed information about the birds on mainland New Zealand and its offshore islands, the reader is referred to the author's *Reed Field Guide to New Zealand Birds*. Readers seeking information on our native trees should refer to J.T. Salmon's *Reed Field Guide to New Zealand Native Trees*. Those books, and others on invertebrates, are available from good bookshops.

I wish to express my appreciation to Ian Watt and Ray Richards for their encouragement in the preparation of this book and to my wife Lynnette for her perseverance and composure in assisting with the text. Also, my thanks to Rod Morris for donating his photograph of the stoat on page 55.

GEOFF MOON

INTRODUCTION

It is estimated that the islands which comprise New Zealand gradually began to separate from the super-continent Gondwanaland more than 80 million years ago.

At the time of this prehistoric isolation, land mammals and snakes had not yet inhabited Gondwanaland. However, the ancestors of some of our birds, reptiles and invertebrates occupied the land that is now New Zealand, before the separation from the supercontinent occurred. It is also possible that, at some later date, birds flew to these islands before the Tasman Sea reached its present width. Later, bats arrived, which are our only endemic terrestrial mammals.

Since that time, New Zealand's topography has been continually altered by vulcanism, erosion, and — during the Ice Ages — glaciation. During this period of transition many unique plants and animals evolved from the original ancient lineage. Although some species have since become extinct, others still make up the special flora and fauna of these islands.

The ratite birds, notably kiwi and the extinct moa, are thought to have occupied a place which in other countries would have been filled by browsing mammals. Similarly, the flightless giant weta, with their vegetarian diet and nocturnal habits, have filled the role normally performed by small rodents.

The tuatara, now present only on predator-free offshore islands, is thought to be little changed since the time it existed with dinosaurs.

Our endemic frogs and some of our geckos exhibit very primitive characteristics, and similarly, our large carnivorous snails are relics of the Gondwanaland fauna.

About 1000 years ago the first human settlers arrived in New Zealand from Polynesia. They found a land heavily forested and teeming with birdlife. As they needed land for planting their crops they felled and burned much of the forest on the east coasts of both the North and South Islands. There is evidence that many of these fires were uncontrolled, devastating large areas.

Those early Maori settlers brought from their ancestral islands the kiore, a small Polynesian rat, and the kuri, a dog. The rats are still present on Stewart Island and some offshore islands. Unlike the rats introduced later by Europeans, kiore are vegetarian, but there is recent evidence that they sometimes prey upon eggs and fledgling birds. Kuri were used for hunting, and some undoubtedly escaped into the wild and fed on flightless birds. Besides eliminating many species of moa, the Maori hunters and their dogs were responsible for the extinction of at least a dozen other bird species.

The tuatara is the only representative of an extinct order of reptiles which existed over 200 million years ago.

According to the palaeontologist and ornithologist Sir Charles Fleming, writing in Volume 1 of *New Zealand's Nature Heritage*: 'The arrival of Polynesian man in New Zealand, together with his dog and rat and his knowledge of fire, brought about changes in New Zealand ecology more severe than any of the violent fluctuations of climate that had taken place since the first Ice Age, some 1,750,000 years ago.'

But the arrival of settlers from Europe had a far more devastating effect on the New Zealand environment. The newcomers required timber for building, and cleared land to create pastures for grazing the domestic animals they brought with them. Much of the forest cutting and burning was unnecessarily ruthless and in steep high country it caused rapid rainwater run-off which eroded hillsides and flooded lowland areas. However, in spite of this destruction, there are still places where magnificent areas of forest remain intact.

The early settlers brought in several species of exotic plants, many of which thrived in the favourable climate. But they also introduced browsing animals, notably deer, pigs, goats and possums. The result was increased destruction of the forests. Possums, which fed on selected plants, damaged shrubs and canopy trees, often completely denuding them, while grazing deer and goats, as well as pigs rooting on the forest floor, prevented regeneration of the trees. Introduced rabbits and hares damaged native vegetation in some high country areas and had a devastating effect on farm pastures.

In an attempt to control the rabbits, stoats and ferrets were brought in. But the abundant birdlife, which had evolved in an environment free from mammalian predators, became easy prey for those mustelids.

In addition, some domestic cats became feral and preyed on both large and small birds.

Several species of European birds were also imported. Many of them were seed eaters, while others fed in orchards and gardens on invertebrates and fruit. They probably did not compete with native species for food, but they did bring disease organisms, to which the native birds, living in isolation, had no immunity. The result was that some native bird species were almost eliminated in some areas.

An example of this occurred in the forests of

Pre-historic Tmesipteris ferns still survive in our forests today, often growing from the trunks of tree ferns.

Auckland's Waitakere Ranges towards the end of last century. These forests had supported good populations of honey-eating birds which disappeared over a short period. The decline was too rapid to have been caused by predators and it is thought that an introduced avian disease was responsible. Today, these forests have been repopulated by tui, which are strong fliers, but bellbirds, which do not migrate, are still absent from the region. However, bird species other than the honey-eaters were not thought to have been affected at the time, as populations of New Zealand pigeons, and small insectivorous birds, such as tomtits and fantails, still inhabit these rapidly regenerating forests.

Owing to the presence of mammalian predators and introduced diseases, many animal populations on the mainland were completely eliminated and certain species only survived on some of the offshore islands.

Two forest birds saved from extinction in this way are the North Island saddleback and the stitchbird, both of which disappeared from mainland forests late last century. It is unlikely that the attractive, lively saddleback can ever be reintroduced to mainland forests, as it feeds on the forest floor where it becomes easy prey for mustelids, feral cats and rats. Fortunately, a small population of saddlebacks survived on predator-free Taranga, or Hen Island, in the northern Hauraki Gulf. Birds transferred to nearby islands have thrived and bred successfully, with the result that today saddlebacks are no longer endangered.

Similarly, rugged, forest-covered Little Barrier Island was the last refuge of the stitchbird, which, like the tui and the bellbird, is a honey-eater. Even here its population was limited by the presence of feral cats. Following a successful cat eradication programme,

INTRODUCTION 15

The largest stands of remaining podocarp forests survive at Pureora and Whirinaki.

completed by the Wildlife Service in 1980, the numbers of stitchbirds have increased so remarkably that it has been possible to transfer birds to other island sanctuaries.

A large proportion of the New Zealand landscape today consists of grassland, arable land and orchards, environments which support a variety of wildlife. In some parts of the country, the lowland and hill country pastures are devoid of native trees, but large areas of native forest do still exist. Some forests are regenerating following earlier logging; others are, as yet, untouched by humans. None of these forests remains in a pristine state; all, to a lesser or greater extent, have been modified by introducing browsing animals, particularly the Australian possum.

New Zealand's remaining forests are unique in character and contain many beautiful and unusual

Puketi forest in Northland

plants and animals. As the islands of New Zealand lie in a wide latitudinal range the climatic variations are often considerable, both in rainfall and temperature. This factor, plus variations in soil types and altitude, have all influenced the growth of our forests. Among the most important areas are the impressive kauri forests of Northland, the ancient podocarp forests of other regions, notably Whirinaki and Pureora, and the extensive stands of rainforest and beech in Westland and Fiordland.

The ancestors of many of our trees, such as the podocarps and beeches, existed in Gondwanaland. One of our tallest native trees, the kahikatea, is a podocarp belonging to the subgenus *Dacrycarpus*, which was present in Gondwana more than 100 million years ago. The podocarps are distinct in bearing a seed attached to a fleshy fruit much sought after by birds.

A characteristic of the New Zealand forests is the large variety of shrubs and ferns growing beneath the canopy of larger trees. On the forest floor, hidden among the mosses, fungi and leaf litter, lives a myriad of invertebrates. These provide food to sustain many species of wildlife and contribute to the chain supporting the ecosystem.

This book describes and illustrates the most obvious and interesting fauna to be found in New Zealand's forest environments. It examines the habitat and depicts the wildlife typical of it.

Some species of animal favour several habitats. For example, the primitive native Hochstetter's frog may

Top, opposite
The enclosed nest of a nuseryweb spider contains the young spiders.

Below, opposite
An endemic short-tailed bat.

Below
Leiopelma frogs are of very ancient lineage and exhibit many primitive characteristics.

be found not only in wet forest locations but also in drier areas, and at high altitudes. Some spider species live in forests, open country and swamplands, while a few birds, notably the New Zealand kingfisher, inhabit open country, the coast and the depths of forests.

It is possible to observe wildlife easily and explore most habitats with little restriction on accessibility. The largest forests today are protected as national and forest parks, and most are freely accessible and provided with excellent tracks. Many also have accommodation huts maintained by the Department of Conservation, from whom maps and information can be obtained. Our forests provide wonderful natural areas where both New Zealanders and tourists can explore and experience our wildlife.

New Zealand

FOREST
and its
Wildlife

New Zealand's evergreen forests range from the kauri forests of Northland to the extensive beech forests of Fiordland. In many regions there is a mix of broadleaf, beech and hardwood trees, while, particularly in the central and south-east areas of the North Island, there are pristine forests of ancient podocarp trees.

In many forests there is evidence of the destruction of foliage by the introduced Australian brush-tailed possum. Feral goats, pigs and deer are also causing damage and hindering forest regeneration. Possums (their number estimated to be at least 70 million), pose a particularly serious problem, as they are selective feeders, devouring foliage and fruits which form the staple diet of many bird species. It has been found recently that they also take birds' eggs and probably their young. Birds and their nests, lizards

Previous page
Kauri forest.

Below
Mixed beech forest in the Kaimanawa Ranges.

and the larger insects are the targets of introduced mustelids, particularly stoats, and also of feral cats.

During much of the day, mainland New Zealand forests are quiet and there is little sign of wildlife. The tranquillity is interrupted by the occasional calls of the tui or the short melodious song of the smaller

Mixed kauri and broadleaf forest.

South Island beech forest.

Below
Westland rainforest.

Left
Regenerating forest in the Waitakere Ranges.

Puriri trees provide nectar-bearing flowers and fruit throughout the year.

bellbird, one of the few birds whose song can be heard at any time of day throughout all months of the year. Its true bell song is heard at its best and purest in early morning.

The lower canopy of small trees and shrubs is favoured by small insectivorous birds. The most noticeable is the fantail, a small flycatcher which often flits about close to humans seeking the insects they may disturb.

Left
The bellbird's song can be heard throughout the year.

Below
The tui is mainly a nectar feeder but also eats fruits and insects.

Tomtits, grey warblers and silvereyes are often seen in the lower canopy, whereas whiteheads and yellowheads, often in family groups, usually feed in the upper canopy of the forest and are sometimes difficult to see.

The migrant long-tailed cuckoo uses the nests of the whitehead and yellowhead in which to lay its eggs, whereas the smaller shining cuckoo chooses the tiny grey warbler to incubate its eggs and foster its chicks.

Right
Fantails are common in forests throughout New Zealand.

Below
A male South Island tomtit.

New Zealand's smallest bird, the rifleman, only 8 cm in length, is commonest in beech forests, particularly at higher altitudes. Another small endemic bird, the brown creeper, is common in South Island lowland forest and scrub, as well as being found at higher altitudes.

The chaffinch, the most common of the introduced

Left
The rifleman, our smallest bird, prefers beech forest habitats.

Below
The shining cuckoo winters in the Solomon Islands. It migrates to New Zealand each spring and lays its eggs in grey warbler nests.

finch species, has spread to all parts of the country, even to remote offshore islands, and is the only finch to be found in the depths of native forests.

Perhaps the most confiding forest bird is the robin. One is often unaware of its presence as it perches close by, watching for food. If leaf litter is disturbed on the forest floor, the robin will dart down to pick up insects which are often too small for the human eye to detect.

The endemic New Zealand pigeon is another bird which can be approached closely when it is feeding or perched. Pigeons favour the mixed podocarp and broadleaf habitats which provide them with a wealth of fruits and foliage. They are uncommon in pure beech forests where their preferred foods are scarce. Pigeons play an important part in the regeneration of forest trees and shrubs. They feed on the fruits of many species. The flesh of the fruit is digested, while the hard seed passes in the birds' droppings to be distributed some distance from the donor tree.

The tiny grey warbler is common in forests and scrub.

A North Island robin.

Feeding on fruits of many species of trees and shrubs, the New Zealand pigeon disperses seeds to maintain forest regeneration.

Right
The whitehead occurs only in the North Island.

Below
A New Zealand pigeon.

The hard seeds of beech trees, although sought after by mice and rats, are unpalatable to birds and disperse only slowly, usually by being washed away after heavy rain.

New Zealand has comparatively few insects capable of pollinating the flowers of its trees and shrubs. However, that function is performed by the nectar-feeding birds — tui, bellbirds, stitchbirds and silvereyes. Also, it has recently been discovered that our only endemic land mammal, the nocturnal short-tailed bat, which is mainly an insect feeder, also pollinates some flowers.

During the day, bats roost in colonies, hanging upside down in selected hollow trees. They leave these roosts at dusk and, with an erratic flight, hawk flying insects above the forest canopy and along its margins.

Some New Zealand kingfishers inhabit forests and bore nesting-holes in rotting trees.

They also hunt insects by crawling along branches, tree fern trunks and the forest floor.

The harsh rattling cry of the kaka, a large parrot, is often heard as it flies above the canopy. It also has a vocabulary of soft flute-like calls and mewings. Kaka are omnivorous, feeding on fruits, foliage, nectar, insects and grubs. They are particularly fond of the grubs of the huhu beetle which bore into dead trees. They extract them by tearing away the wood with their powerful hooked beaks. Kaka are dependent on mature forests for nesting. They may obtain food from regenerating forests but only mature forests can meet their needs fully, as it is the mature trees which provide the dry cavities for their nests. Kakariki, the small red-crowned and yellow-crowned parakeets, also require mature forest for feeding and nesting in cavities of large trees.

Kaka inhabit large tracts of forest where they nest in cavities of large trees.

Above
The grubs of the huhu beetle are found in dead trees. They are a favourite food of the kaka.

Left
The red-crowned parakeet is becoming scarce in mainland forests but is common on many offshore islands.

The endangered kokako, a bird of ancient lineage related to the saddleback and the now extinct huia, is still present in small numbers in some North Island forests, particularly Puketi Forest in Northland and Pureora Forest, west of Lake Taupo.

A North Island kokako.

The kokako is a weak flier. With its strong legs it moves through the forest by springing from branch to branch, using its rounded wings to maintain balance and to glide between trees.

Kokako are mainly vegetarian, their diet varying with the seasons. In late summer and autumn they feed on foliage and fruits of podocarp and hardwood trees and on berries from a variety of shrubs and vines. They eat insects during the warmer months and especially when chicks need to be fed on a richer protein diet.

Although kokako often feed on the forest floor, they are usually difficult to see as they spend much of their time hidden in the upper canopy of tall trees. They are renowned for their hauntingly beautiful song, which consists of long, mellow, euphonious notes, followed by clear flute-like passages and repeated clucks and mews. The song is best heard soon after dawn.

Kiwi are unlikely to be seen during daylight hours, except perhaps Stewart Island kiwi, which often

The North Island kokako survives precariously in remnants of mature forest. Some birds have been relocated to predator-free offshore islands.

emerge from their burrows well before dusk or even during the day when the weather is dull. The rather plaintive call of the male kiwi can be heard in many forested areas and in scrub country in Northland. The call of the male consists of a series of ascending and descending whistles (ki-wi); in contrast, the female utters a shorter, hoarse cry. Kiwi eat a variety of invertebrates and berries which have fallen to the ground. In their search for earthworms, they use their long bills to probe deeply into the soil, leaving telltale conical holes in areas of moist soil.

Another nocturnal forest bird is the morepork, our only surviving endemic species of owl. Morepork are often visible during daylight hours, perhaps perched under a tree fern or in another shady spot.

Brown kiwis inhabit forests; in Northland they are found in scrub and pine plantations.

If they venture into the open they are mobbed by smaller birds until forced to find another secluded resting place. Although normally forest dwellers, moreporks have adapted to the changed environment and now frequent parks and farmland, provided there are clumps of trees for roosting and nesting.

Although mainly forest inhabitants, moreporks have adapted to living in more open country, so long as there are trees to provide shelter and nesting sites.

The New Zealand falcon, sometimes called the bush hawk, inhabits forested regions of Westland and the southern half of the North Island, as well as high country habitats. Unlike our other diurnal raptor, the harrier, the falcon is not a scavenger and takes only live prey, diving at high speed to strike small birds in mid-air.

Birds are the most conspicuous inhabitants of the forests, but there are innumerable other small creatures which fit into the ecological chain. Many species of invertebrates provide food for birds, lizards, bats, the praying mantis and the large carnivorous kauri snail.

Right
Short-tailed bats catch insects on the wing. They also pollinate flowers when feeding on nectar.

Below
Shells of kauri snails. There are approximately forty species of these carnivorous snails inhabiting moist areas of forest throughout New Zealand.

Many creatures remain hidden, while others rely on camouflage to escape predation. For example, the cryptic coloration of the common forest gecko blends remarkably with the bark of a tree or branch, while the green of other species of gecko accurately matches the foliage of the shrubs on which they rest. Many forest birds are dull coloured and often it is only their movement or sound which brings them to our attention.

A forest gecko camouflaged on a tree trunk.

Top *A green gecko of the genus* Naultinus.

Bottom *A common forest gecko.*

Many creatures remain in holes in trees, under loose bark or beneath the leaves on the forest floor. Shiny-skinned skinks hide under stones or fallen logs, but they sometimes venture out to bask in shafts of sunlight which filter to the forest floor, where they may fall victim to sharp-eyed kingfishers. However, skinks have the ability to shed their tails when attacked. The vigorous wriggling of this tail portion often succeeds in distracting the predator while the skink makes its escape. The tail later regrows.

Many species of insect live in the forest and a great number of the smaller ones are yet to be named and classified. Some of the most interesting endemic insects are the wingless weta. These are vegetarians, although some will scavenge the remains of dead insects, and all are nocturnal in habit. Weta belong to an ancient group of insects, and because New Zealand has long been isolated from other

A common copper skink.

lands and had no small terrestrial mammals, they are considered to have filled an ecological niche normally occupied by small rodents.

The large kauri snail is also nocturnal, coming out

A common weta. Weta are vegetarian and feed at night.

Left and below
Stick insects are vegetarian. They are a favourite food of moreporks, kingfishers and tuis.

after dark for earthworms and insects among the leaf litter.

Stick insects, a favourite food of many birds, choose backgrounds to suit their coloration. Green ones rest on foliage and brown ones, except when feeding, rest on branches. They are difficult to see as their twig-like bodies resemble the twigs on which they pose.

The German and common wasps are introduced insects that pose a threat to native wildlife. Not only do they feed on insects, including large stick insects, but, in parts of the South Island, they consume honeydew from the trunks of beech trees — a food much sought after by kaka and bellbirds.

Several of New Zealand's more than 30 species of cicada inhabit the forest. The larger varieties were once used as food by the Maori. Each species has a

The puriri moth is the largest endemic moth.

different dialect, and the crackling crescendo of song is especially noticeable on hot summer days. Cicadas are frequently seen resting on foliage or stems where they feed on the sap of plants. During its larval stage the cicada spends several years underground, feeding on the roots of plants. The nymph stage eventually emerges to crawl up a tree trunk, shedding its skin to become a winged adult. Cicada nymphs are a favourite food of kiwi.

New Zealand has few species of butterfly but there are more than 1500 different moths. Butterflies are usually seen in open country, although the admiral butterflies favour forest margins where they seek out ongaonga, or stinging nettle, on which to lay their eggs. Many moth species inhabit the forest, the most spectacular of them being the large puriri moth. The wingspan of females may be up to 15 cm.

Several species of nurseryweb spider of the genus Dolomedes inhabit forest, open country and swamps. The egg sac is carried by the female until a silken nursery web is constructed to contain the newly hatched spiders.

The caterpillars feed on the wood of puriri trees, the burrows being often about 30 cm long. The caterpillar stage may last up to four years. When the moth finally emerges, it does not feed but only lives long enough to breed.

There are several species of spider that inhabit forest areas. Some build webs of differing shapes in which to entangle their prey, while others, such as the wolf and nurseryweb spiders, capture insects by jumping on them. Tunnelweb spiders occupy small holes in trees or under loose bark, using a small amount of web around the entrance. This acts as a device for

A primitive Hochstetter's frog, showing the partially webbed hind toes.

detecting any insect which may stray that way. Several different species of orbweb spiders build their circular webs in forest clearings or between shrubs on the forest margins to capture flying insects.

New Zealand has three species of primitive frog of very ancient lineage. All are small, measuring no more than 50 mm in length. They occupy a wide range of habitats, from forest streams to rocky areas at high altitudes. All are nocturnal and feed on small insects and grubs.

Archey's frog is the smallest species and inhabits part of the Coromandel Ranges. Hochstetter's frog is widely distributed from East Cape northwards, including the Coromandel Ranges. It can be distinguished from Archey's frog by its partially webbed hind toes.

The praying mantis is carnivorous and preys on other insects.

Several species of cicada inhabit the forest. Where there are trees, they will also live in open country.

To date, all publications describing the life cycles of these endemic frogs have said that eggs are laid inside gelatinous capsules, and that embryos develop into froglets with tails, there being no free-swimming tadpole stage. However, this information appears to be debatable, at least in relation to the breeding of Hochsetter's frog in a wet Northland locality.

Recent observations, supported by photographs, show
that the tadpoles emerged from the capsules and
swam freely in small pools of water beneath rocks
close to a stream. They remained at that tadpole stage

Left
An Australian brush-tailed possum.

Below
Stoats were originally introduced to New Zealand to control rabbits. They are now a serious threat to our bird life.

for a few weeks before developing into tailed froglets, the tails then being gradually absorbed.

The third of the natives, Hamilton's frog, is the rarest. It is found only in very localised areas on Stephens and Maud Islands.

The New Zealand native forests provide vital habitats for many species of wildlife, both seen and unseen.

Right
Brown creepers are found in high altitude scrub as well as in lowland forests and scrub.

Below
Chaffinches are the only species of finch to inhabit both forest and open country.

A red-crowned parakeet pair at a nest hole.

More nectar-feeding birds and insects live in the warmer districts of the north, while the cooler beech forests attract a greater proportion of insectivorous birds.

Within all these forest regions there is a special ecology, with each animal being important and dependent on the others in the continuation of the cycle of forest life.

North Island robin at nest.

Montane South Island beech forest.

Orbweb spiders spin their webs on fences or between branches of shrubs to capture insects.

INDEX

admiral butterfly 51
Archey's frog 53
bat, short-tailed 10, 19, 35–36, 44
bellbird 14, 27, 35, 50
brown creeper 29, 56
bush hawk *see* falcon
butterflies 51
cat (feral) 13, 14, 23
chaffinch 29–30, 56
cicada 50–51, 54
common wasp 50
Coromandel Ranges 53
cuckoo
   long-tailed 28
   shining 28, 29
deer 12, 22
falcon (New Zealand) 43
fantail 14, 27, 28
ferret 12
Fiordland 17, 22
Fleming, Sir Charles 12
frog 10, 18, 53–56
   Archey's 53
   Hamilton's 56
   Hochstetter's 17–18, 52, 53, 54–56
gecko 10, 45, 46
German wasp 50

goat 12, 22
Gondwanaland 10, 17
grey warbler 28, 30
Hamilton's frog 56
hare 12
harrier (Australasian) 43
hawk *see* harrier
Hen Island (Taranga) 14
high country 12
Hochstetter's frog 17–18, 52, 53, 54–56
huhu 36, 37
huia 38
islands, offshore 14, 30
Kaimanawa Ranges 22
kaka 36, 50
kakariki (parakeet) 36, 37, 57
kauri snail 44, 48–50
kingfisher 18, 35, 47
kiore 11
kiwi 10, 40–41, 51
kokako 38–40
kuri 11
Little Barrier Island 14
lizard 22, 44
moa 10, 11
morepork 41–43
moths 51

INDEX

mountain parrot *see* kea

Northland 17, 22, 38, 41

nurseryweb spider 19, 52

offshore islands 14, 30

orbweb spider 53, 60–61

pig 12, 22

pigeon (New Zealand) 14, 30, 32–35

possum (Australian) 12, 16, 22, 55

praying mantis 44, 53

Puketi Forest 16, 38

Pureora Forest 17, 38

puriri moth 50, 51–52

rabbit 12

rat, Polynesian *see* kiore

rifleman 29

robin, North Island 30, 31, 58

stoat 12, 23, 55

tomtit 14, 28

tuatara 10, 11

tui 14, 23, 27, 35

tunnelweb spider 52–53

Waitakere Ranges 14, 25

wasp
  common 50
  German 50

Westland 17, 25, 43

weta 10, 47–48

Whirinaki Forest 17

whitehead 28, 34

wolf spider 52

yellowhead 28

saddleback (North Island) 14, 38

silvereye 28, 35

skink 47

snail 10

spider 18, 51, 52
  nurseryweb 19, 52
  orbweb 53, 60–61
  tunnelweb 52–53
  wolf 52

Stephens Island 56

Stewart Island 40

stitchbird 14, 16, 35

stick insect 49, 50

NORTH ISLAND

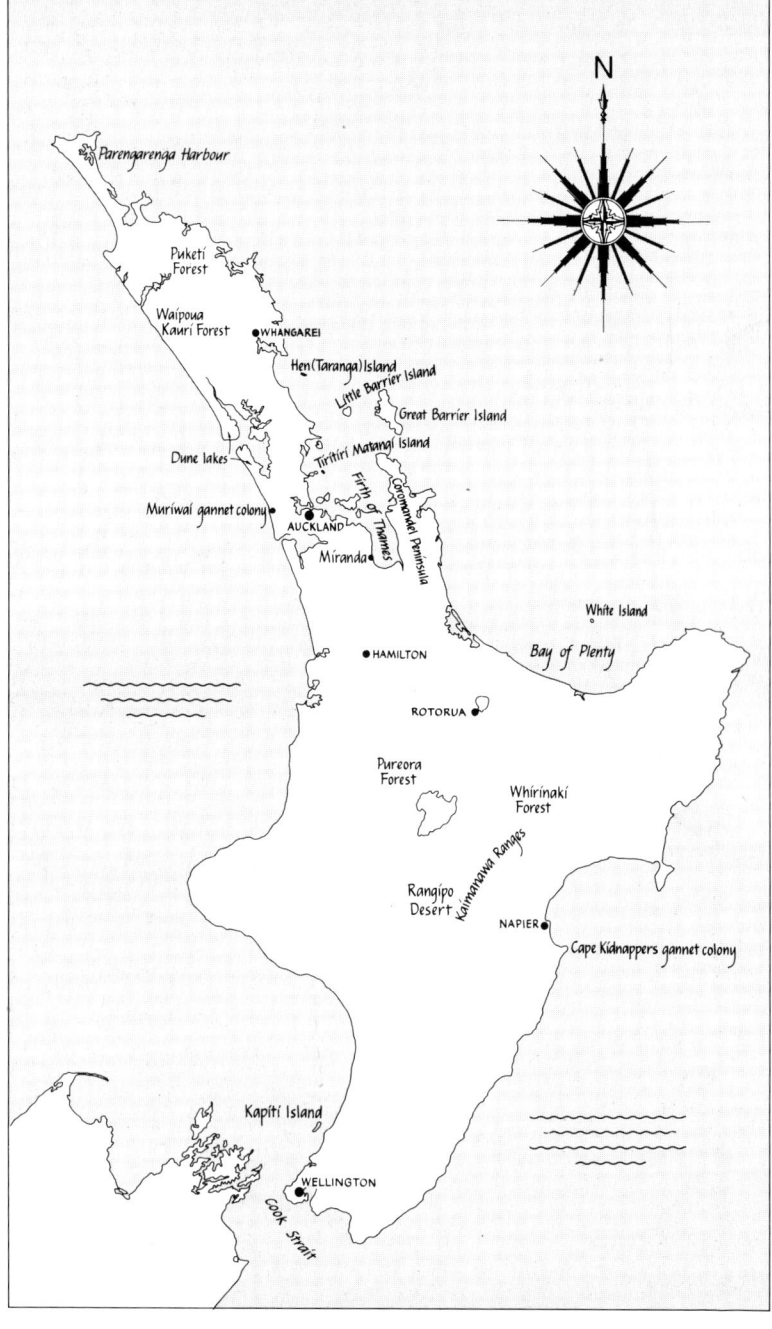